Mature Audiences Only

When I wake up,
my best friends
are right there
next to me

When we go anywhere, we go as a three

Hello!

I help them feel
better when
they're feeling blue

Our home is cosy
and warm,
we like a tidy yard

It's a bit of a squeeze when we try to sit on a chair

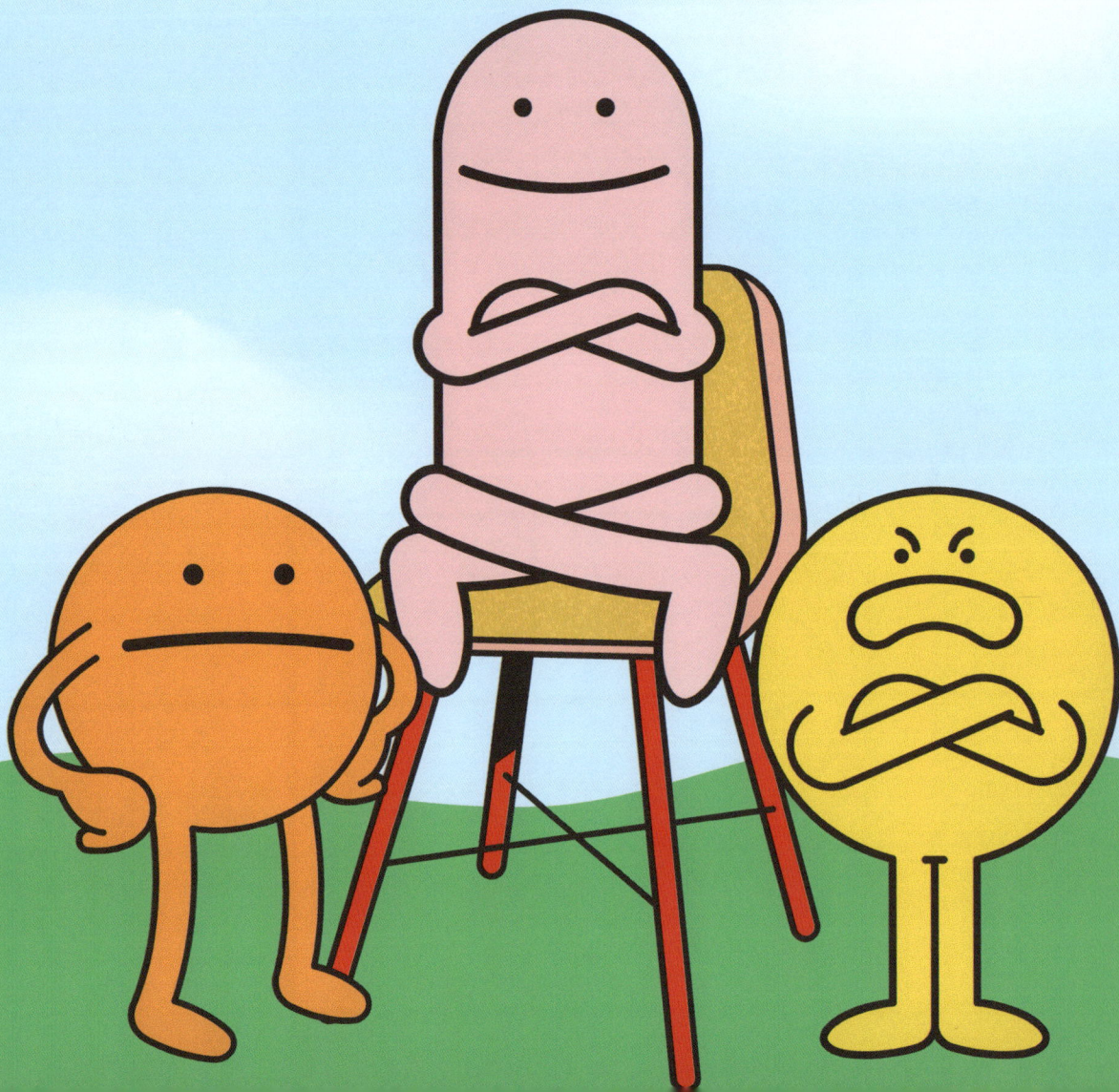

My best friends can grow some really curly hair!

Sometimes we all get kisses,
and that's very nice!

We can all look smaller when it's as cold as ice!

But, we love playing games, like hide and seek!

My friends can
get itchy
and need a good
scratch

They laugh when I put my hat on and watch me struggle!

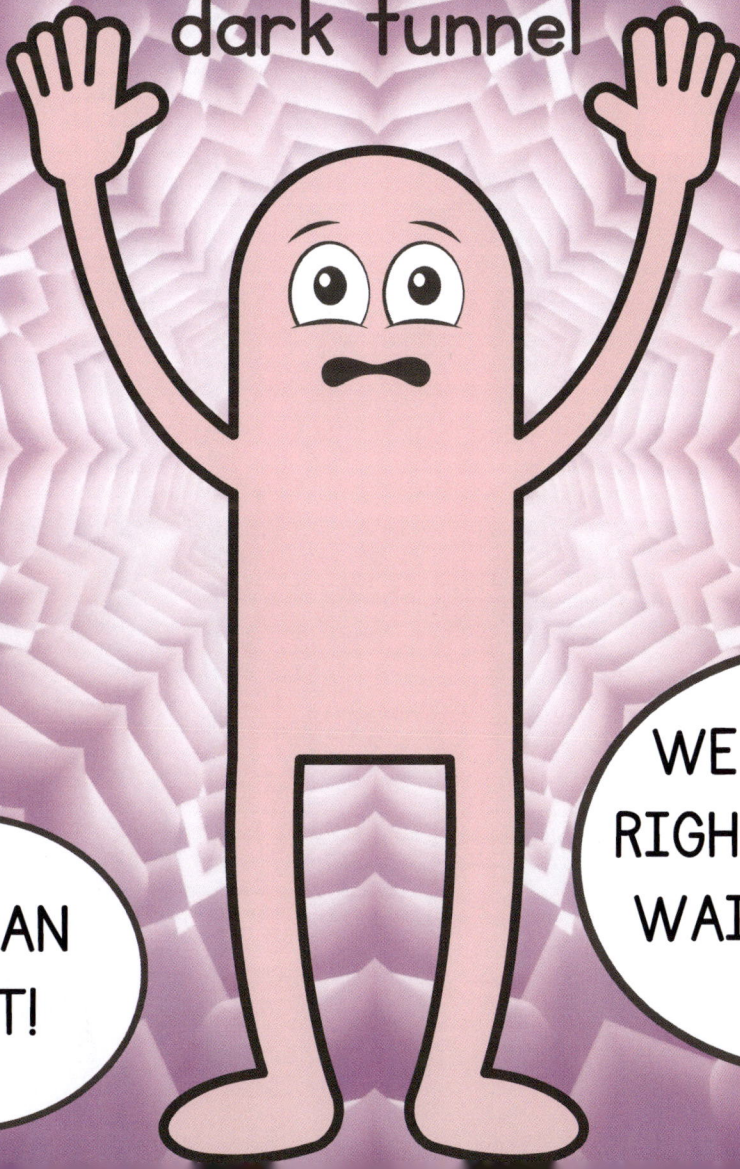

Despite their bad points, they are my besties. It's true!

One to the left, the other to the right. Stuck together like glue!

# The End

# About The Author
# Jen Jenivive

Has excellent ball skills.
Lover of silly, immature humour

@jenjenivivereads

@jenjenivivereads

@jenjenivive

www.jenjenivive.com

# Other Titles Include:

## For full book collection visit www.jenjenivive.com

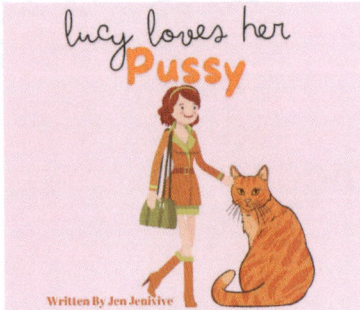

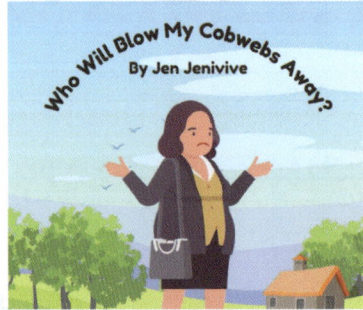

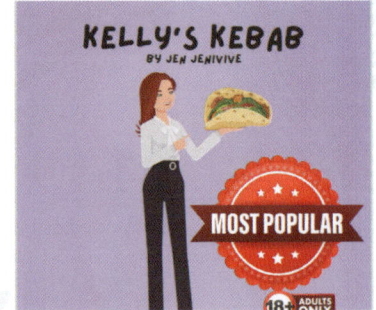

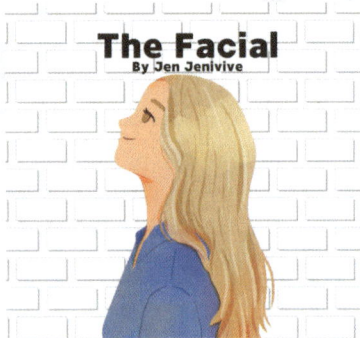

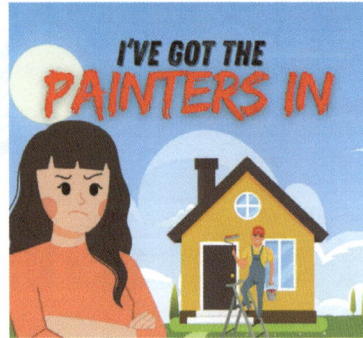

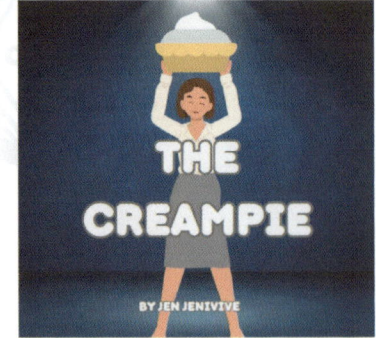

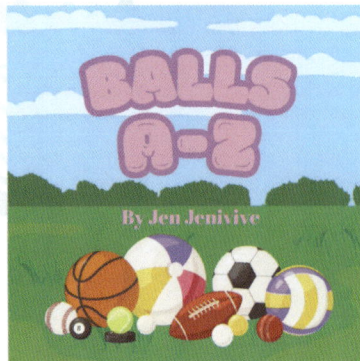

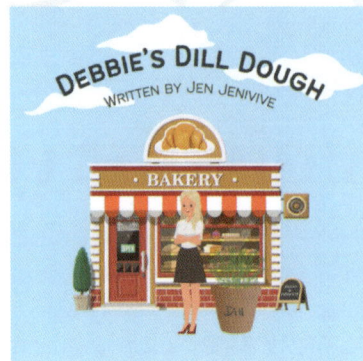

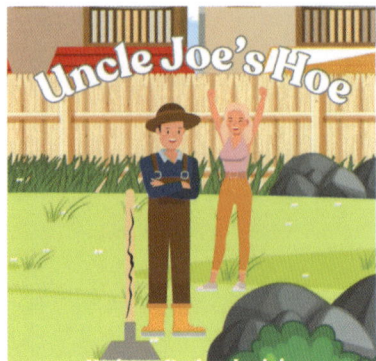

lucy loves her **Pussy**
Written By Jen Jenivive

Who Will Blow My Cobwebs Away?
By Jen Jenivive

KELLY'S KEBAB
BY JEN JENIVIVE
MOST POPULAR
18+ ADULTS ONLY

The Facial
By Jen Jenivive

I'VE GOT THE PAINTERS IN

THE CREAMPIE
BY JEN JENIVIVE

BALLS A-Z
By Jen Jenivive

DEBBIE'S DILL DOUGH
WRITTEN BY JEN JENIVIVE
BAKERY

Uncle Joe's Hoe

Printed in Great Britain
by Amazon